TIME FOR KIDS READERS

AF271367

THE PONY EXPRESS

by Renee Skelton

Harcourt
SCHOOL PUBLISHERS

Orlando   Austin   New York   San Diego   Toronto   London

Visit *The Learning Site!*
www.harcourtschool.com

In St. Joseph, Missouri, on April 3, 1860, a crowd gathered in the middle of town. Why? A new mail service called the Pony Express was about to begin there. If it worked, it would do something that had never been done. It would get mail from Missouri to California in 10½ days.

Today that is slow. But in 1860, letters and news took weeks to cross the country.

In 1860 most people in the United States lived east of the Mississippi River. A wilderness almost 2,000 miles wide separated them from the settlements in California. Today we have cars, trains, and airplanes. But in 1860, there wasn't any fast or easy way to cross the country.

The Pony Express captured the imagination of Americans.

The Pony Express Gets Started

By 1860, the U.S. government had set up several mail delivery routes to California. One route took the mail by ship from New York to Panama. Mules or stagecoaches carried it across Panama. Then another ship took the mail up the Pacific coast to San Francisco. Another route brought mail overland through Tennessee, Missouri, and Texas, to California. But even the fastest delivery by land took at least three weeks.

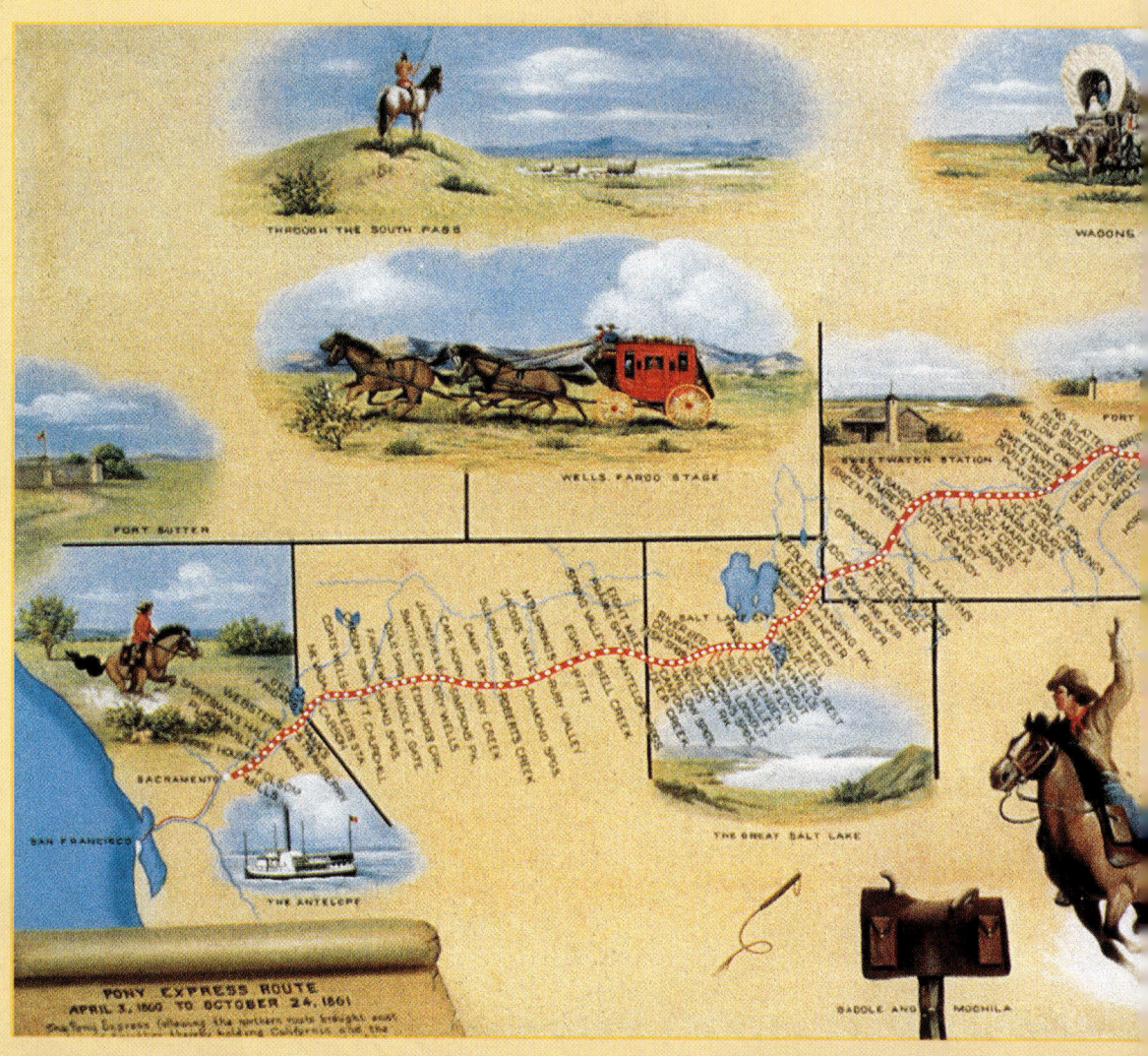

People across the country were excited about the Pony Express. Riders would speed across the land, carrying the mail. A chain of Pony Express stations crossed the Great Plains and the Rocky Mountains. No one knew if it would work.

St. Joseph was the western end of the railroad line. So, the Pony Express route started there. The mail arrived in St. Joseph from the East. Then the Pony Express would carry it by horseback to California.

This map shows a route of the Pony Express from Missouri to California.

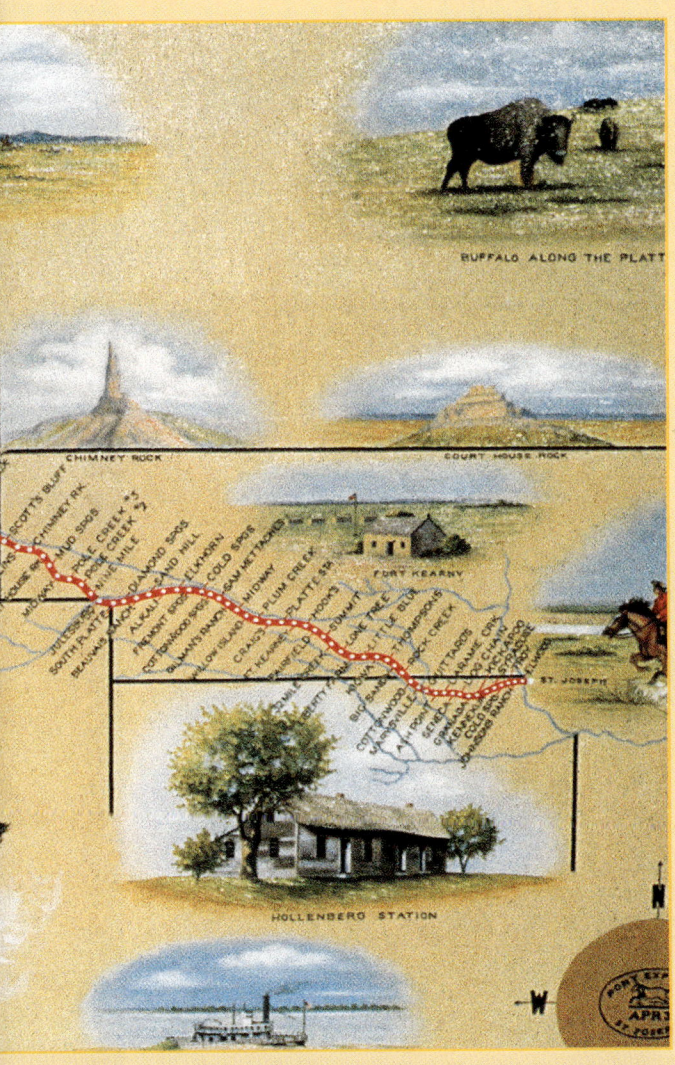

BUFFALO ALONG THE PLATT

CHIMNEY ROCK

COURT HOUSE ROCK

FORT KEARNY

ST. JOSEPH

HOLLENBERG STATION

TFK SPOTLIGHT

BRONCHO CHARLIE:
YOUNGEST RIDER

In July 1861, Broncho Charlie made his first ride for the Pony Express. He was just 11 years old. Broncho Charlie worked for the Pony Express for only a few months because it ended its run in October 1861. He lived to the age of 81, and he loved to talk about his exciting rides.

The First Run

By late afternoon on April 3, the mail train was already hours late. Finally, the crowds heard the train whistle. The train pulled in, and clerks quickly took the mail from it. They put the mail in the leather *mochila*, or mailbag, of Johnny Frey. Frey was the first Pony Express rider. On that first ride, Frey carried 49 letters and several telegrams.

The boom of a cannon sounded in the early evening. Frey leaped onto his horse. He galloped to the edge of the Missouri River. A ferry took Frey and his horse across. On the other side Frey took off in a cloud of dust. He headed west across Kansas. He traveled about 75 miles. He changed horses several times. At his last stop, Frey handed the mochila to the next rider.

Two thousand miles away, crowds gathered in Sacramento, California. It was the western end of the Pony Express route. The western mail would start in San Francisco. It would go up the Sacramento River to Sacramento. From there, Pony Express riders would take the mail east.

A few hours after Frey left St. Joseph, Sam Hamilton left Sacramento. He left at 2:45 A.M. on April 4. He carried the mail east. Hamilton changed horses twice during the night. At about 8:00 A.M. he reached a station near the Sierra Nevada.

a mochila

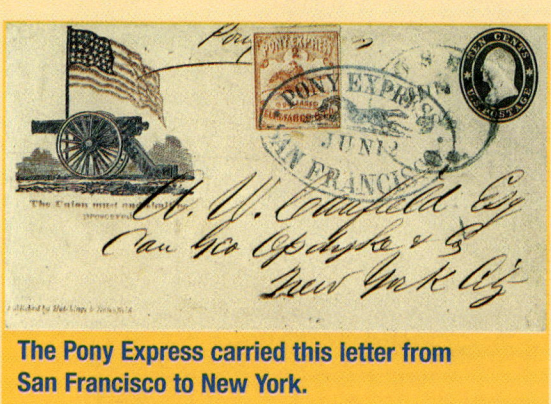

The Pony Express carried this letter from San Francisco to New York.

Johnny Frey

TFK SPOTLIGHT

JOHNNY FREY:

FIRST IN THE SADDLE

Johnny Frey was the perfect person to be a Pony Express rider. He was young and small, weighing less than 120 pounds. Frey was also a fast rider. Before he became a Pony Express rider, he raced horses. Frey didn't work for the Pony Express for very long. When the Civil War began, Frey volunteered for the Union Army. He died in a battle at Baxter Springs, Kansas.

In less than two minutes, Warren Upson took the mochila from Hamilton. Upson then traveled east from the station. Snow fell hard as Upson crossed the Sierra Nevada.

The snow covered the trail, making it hard for him to find his way. At times Upson had to walk in the snow, leading his horse. Finally, Upson reached a station on the other side of the mountains. There he passed the mail to the next rider.

Pony Express riders had to travel through snowstorms.

On April 8, the eastbound and westbound Pony Express riders met in Utah, near Salt Lake City. The eastbound mail reached St. Joseph on the afternoon of April 13. A huge celebration greeted the rider. The westbound mail got to Sacramento on April 14 at 1:00 A.M. Still, 2,000 people met the mail. The Pony Express worked. Mail had crossed the country in 10½ days.

This was good news for both the country and for the private company that ran the Pony Express— the Central Overland California and Pikes Peak Express Company. The company hoped to make a lot of money if the Pony Express succeeded.

This cartoon shows the people of Sacramento celebrating the arrival of the first Pony Express rider.

1 Number of mail sacks lost by the Pony Express

5 Cost (in dollars) to send one-half ounce of mail by Pony Express

11 Age of youngest Pony Express rider

18 Number of months the Pony Express operated

25 Weekly salary (in dollars) of a Pony Express rider

75 Number of riders needed for one cross-country mail delivery

119 Maximum weight (in pounds) of a Pony Express rider

186 Number of men who rode for the Pony Express

308 Number of Pony Express runs made while the service lasted

34,753 Total number of letters carried by the Pony Express

This letter, delivered by a Pony Express rider, announced the election of Abraham Lincoln.

The Route of the Pony Express

William H. Russell was one of the partners in the company. He wasn't the first to think of carrying mail by horseback across the country, but he was the first to organize a company to do it. His partners were Alexander Majors and William Waddell.

William H. Russell

When Russell and his partners set up their company in January 1860, many people said the Pony Express would fail. The West had only a few settlements. Most of the route would cross thousands of miles of unsettled territory. The American Indians did not want the Pony Express. They did not want more settlers crossing or living on the land.

First the partners had to choose a route. They chose one that followed the Oregon and California trails. These were two of the trails pioneers used to go west.

From St. Joseph, Missouri, the route crossed the plains of what are now Kansas and Nebraska. In western Colorado, it crossed the Rocky Mountains. The route then dropped into the rough hills and deserts of Wyoming, Utah, and Nevada. The last part of the route crossed the rugged Sierra Nevada. Sacramento was its western end.

The route was divided into stages, or sections. The mail traveled almost 2,000 miles, but each rider only went back and forth over the same small section. First the rider would carry the mail across his section one way. After resting, he would take the mail going in the other direction. It took about 75 riders to complete the route across the country.

A rider for the Pony Express arrives at a station in the Rocky Mountains.

The Pony Express Arrives in Sacramento

"First a cloud of rolling dust in the direction of the fort, then a horseman bearing a small flag, riding furiously down J Street, and then a straggling, charging band of horsemen, flying after him, heralding the coming of the Express . . . But out of this confounded confusion, mingled fun and earnestness, emerged at last the Pony Express, trotting up to the door of the agency (Alta Telegraph office) and depositing its precious mail in ten days from St. Joseph to Sacramento. Hip, hip, hurrah for the Pony carrier!"

The Sacramento Daily Union, Sacramento, California April 14, 1860

Riding for the Pony Express

The Pony Express had about 165 stations. Home stations were larger stations. They were 75 to 100 miles apart, at the ends of sections. The mail was transferred at home stations. There were also smaller stations in between the home stations. These stations were 10 to 15 miles apart. Riders got fresh horses at the smaller stations.

After setting up the stations, the company needed fast, strong horses. The Pony Express used about 400 horses. For the flat stretches of the Great Plains, they picked swift, long-legged horses. They chose sturdy animals to cross the hot deserts and rugged mountains.

The riders were the most important part of the Pony Express. They had to be strong, brave, and skilled. Newspaper advertisements asked for thin, strong men not more than 18 years old. The ads said the applicants had to be experts willing to risk death daily. Riders had to weigh less than 120 pounds to keep the load on the horses light. The pay was excellent for the time. They made between $100 and $125 a month. Riders also got free meals and a place to live.

Hundreds of young men applied for the jobs. The Pony Express chose 80. Some were teenagers, but many were about 20 years old. Each rider wore a badge that said Pony Express Messenger. At first, they wore hats, red shirts, and denim pants tucked into boots. Before long, they just wore whatever was comfortable.

When they were not on the job, riders spent their time at home stations on the route. Some home stations were in deserts. Others were on empty plains with nothing in sight. Many stations had dirt floors and rough furniture. The stations were near springs or wells. So, they had plenty of water for riders and horses.

Riders and station keepers often faced danger. Riders faced flooded rivers, blizzards, and desert heat of 100°F. Wolves and mountain lions sometimes attacked them. Bandits chased them. Still, the mail almost always got through.

This letter was sent by Pony Express in 1860.

Richard Egan was a Pony Express rider who once traveled 150 miles through a snowstorm without stopping.

BOB HASLAM:
FASTEST RIDE

Bob Haslam took part in the fastest delivery ever made by the Pony Express. The new U.S. President, Abraham Lincoln, gave his inaugural address in March 1861. People on the West Coast wanted to read the words of the new President. Officials sent the speech by telegraph to Kearney, Nebraska. Then Pony Express riders sped off to California with a copy. The whole trip across the United States took just 7 days and 17 hours—a record time. Haslam rode one 120-mile leg of the trip in about 8 hours.

Buffalo Bill Cody

Wild Bill Hickok

Several legendary Wild West figures rode for the Pony Express. Wild Bill Hickok and Buffalo Bill Cody were Pony Express riders. Cody became a Pony Express rider at the age of 15. Cody set the record for the longest ride. He faced bandits and attacks by American Indians on his route. He became known for his courage and skill as a rider.

Californians depended on the Pony Express. It was the fastest way to get news between the East and West coasts. The Pony Express carried news that told Californians about the election of Abraham Lincoln and the start of the Civil War. When the Civil War blocked the southern mail route, the Pony Express kept communication open to California.

The Pony Express delivered the mail faster than ever before. But it did not last long. Russell, Majors, and Waddell had borrowed hundreds of thousands of dollars to start the Pony Express. They needed money to stay in business. They had hoped for a $1 million contract to take the U.S. mail to California over the central route. However, a different company got the contract.

It was the increased use of the telegraph that ended the Pony Express. The Pacific Telegraph Company finished its line to San Francisco in October 1861. People could send news and messages to California in minutes. They no longer needed the Pony Express.

The coming of the telegraph brought about the end of the Pony Express.

The End of the Pony Express

The Pony Express ended in October 1861, but not before becoming a legend. There is now a Pony Express Museum in St. Joseph, Missouri. Some of the old stations have also been turned into museums. In 1996, when the Olympic torch was carried across the country, it went part of the way on horseback on the old Pony Express route.

In 1860 people were excited when the first rider left for California. Today there's something about the Pony Express that still excites people. Maybe it's the idea of speeding across the wilderness, just a rider and a horse. Do you think you would have wanted to ride for the Pony Express?

A stamp saluting the one-hundredth anniversary of the start of the Pony Express was issued in 1960.